C000162905

NORWICH

Volume 2

A Second Portrait in Old Picture Postcards

by

Philip Standley

S. B. Publications
1989

First published in 1989 by S. B. Publications

5 Queen Margaret's Road, Loggerheads, Nr. Market Drayton, Shropshire, TF9 4EP.

ISBN 1 870708 20 2

Typeset and Printed by Geo. R. Reeve Ltd., Wymondham, Norfolk NR18 0BD.

CONTENTS

CONTENTS CONTINUED

CONTENTS CONTINUED

CONTENTS CONTINUED

Also published by S.B. Publications in the series: "A Portrait in Old Picture Postcards".

Bootle	Norwich Vol. 1	West Norfolk
Bootle Vol. 2	Peterborough	
Liverpool Vol. 1 – The City	Peterborough Vol. 2	
Liverpool Vol. 2 – The Docks and River Mersey	Huntingdon and Godmanchester	
Rock Ferry	The Villages of Old Cambridgeshire	
The Blue Funnel Line	Chesterfield	
Bridgnorth	Chester	The Black Country
Chirk and the Glyn Valley Tramway	Chester Vol 2	Wolverhampton
Oswestry and District		
Shrewsbury		

Other titles in preparation; for full details write to S.B. Publications.

INTRODUCTION

When I was first asked to compile a selection of postcards from my collection for my first book — Norwich, A Portrait in Old Picture Postcards — the publisher and I soon realised that it would be impossible to feature all of the city and its surrounding villages in just one volume.

Following the considerable interest in Volume One, and the many requests for a second volume, I have made a further selection from my own collection, with the help of members of the Norfolk Postcard Club who have kindly loaned postcards from their own collections, to assemble this second nostalgic portrait of the city.

Many of the postcard views have not been published in books before, and I have tried to select as many rare and unusual views as possible, with special emphasis on the surrounding villages and the city's social history.

This book has been designed to follow a route commencing at the Market Place and then following an anti-clockwise tour within and on the boundary of the City walls and featuring street scenes and buildings not included in Volume One. The route then proceeds up Magdalen Road to Sprowston and visits Old Catton, New Catton, Hellesdon, Drayton, Heigham Grove, Costessey, Earlham, the southern suburbs, Trowse, Thorpe Hamlet, Thorpe St. Andrew and Whitlingham. The book concludes with a series of views illustrating local events, disasters, advertisements and humour. Many of the views have been cross-referenced with Volume One.

I would like to take this opportunity to thank the many readers who have written to me expressing their enjoyment of Volume One. These letters often contain valuable pieces of local information which are so very helpful in my research.

I trust that this second volume will give further pleasure to readers and to help relive many happy memories of the "Good Old Days".

Philip Standley
Wymondham
April 1989

ACKNOWLEDGEMENTS

The author is indebted to the following people without whom this book would not have been possible:-

For the loan of various postcards:
Richard Bartram: pages 17, 57, 64, 67, 69, 71, 88, 89, 93 and 96.
Rhoda Bunn: pages 20, 46, 48, 82 and 94.
John Chenery: pages 15, 30, 45 and 59.
Michael Dixon: pages 1, 37, 49, 51, 72, 90, 95, 104, 110 and 113.
Joyce Gurney-Read: page 85.
Basil Gowen: pages 98, 100, 102 and 109.
Nigel Martin: pages 6, 40 and 53.
John Mills: page 80.
Colin Proctor: pages 5, 9, 12, 24, 43, 50, 61, 73, 78 and 99.
Bessie Sewell: pages 112, 115, 116 and 117.
Paul Standley: page 65.
Patricia Willington: pages 21, 79 and 81.
Geoffrey Goreham: page 108.

Typing and additional research: Mary and Sarah Standley.
Editorial and marketing: Steve Benz.

Abbreviations used in text: p.u. – postally used; c – circa.

Postcard collecting has grown in popularity over the last ten years. If you are interested in furthering your knowledge about this fascinating hobby, many clubs now exist to assist collectors.

The Norfolk Postcard Club meets at the Assembly House, Theatre Street, Norwich, on the second Wednesday of every month (except August) at 7 p.m. for 7.30 p.m.. Activities include visits from guest speakers, displays, and postcard dealers in attendance every month.

THE CITY HALL, c. 1937

The City Hall stands in a commanding position above the Market Place, with its 202 ft-high tower visible from all parts of the city.

It was designed by C. H. James and S. Rowland Pierce, who had won the competition for the best design for the new building, with much of the facade modelled on Stockholm's City Hall. The foundation stone was laid in 1936 by the Lord Mayor of Norwich and the building was constructed with greyish-red brick and yellow Ketton stone over three years costing £220,000. The City Hall was officially opened by H.M. King George VI on 29th October, 1938.

The finished building features a 365 ft. balcony, a clock tower housing a three-ton bell, and two bronze heraldic lions, costing £600 each, in front of the main entrance.

This view shows building work still in progress on the site of the War Memorial, and the buildings on the left. In the left background can be seen some of the old buildings which have been replaced by the Norwich Library and the Bethel Street car park.

1

THE R33 AIRSHIP OVER THE GUILDHALL

The R33 airship came into service in 1919 and survived until 1928. It flew for a total of 800 hours — the longest flying time of any British rigid airship. Its sister ship, R34, was the first airship to cross the Atlantic, and both airships were copies of the German naval Zeppelin L33, shot down in September 1916, near Little Wigborough, Essex.

The R33 was based at Pulham airfield, about six miles north-east of Diss. On 16th April 1925, a fierce storm caused severe damage to its nose and the airship broke away from its mooring mast. It drifted over to the North Sea, and going backwards sometimes, the R33 was blown all the way to Holland. Eventually the weather improved for it to be brought back safely after thirty hours in the air. The crew received a message of appreciation from King George V.

Does anybody remember the airship flying over Norwich?

POPE'S HEAD YARD, c. 1912

Pope's Head Yard and the inn of the same name adjoined the Beehive public house in St. Peter's Street, which ran from St. Giles' Street, behind the Municipal Buildings, to Haymarket.

These buildings, along with adjoining properties in St. Peter's Street and the eastern end of Bethel Street, were demolished in 1935 to make way for the building of the City Hall.

The postcard is number 44 from the L.L. series of 58 Norwich cards.

44 NORWICH. — Pope's Head Yard. — LL.

3

St. Peters Mancroft Church, Norwich

HAY HILL, p.u. 1913

Hay Hill is really an extension to the Market Place. In the foreground is the statue to Sir Thomas Browne (1605–82), the author of "Religio Medici" and one of the great prose writers of the 17th century. He was also a physician, practising in Norwich, and was knighted by Charles II in 1671. The statue was designed by Henry Pegram, erected in 1905, and unveiled by Lord Avebury on 19th October, 1905.

In the left background is the brush factory of S. D. Page & Sons, the site formerly occupied by Alderman Riseborough's School for Poor Boys. After Page's brush factory moved to Wymondham in 1920, the building was occupied by Lamberts, tea merchants, and Flinders, electrical wholesalers. The site is now C&A's store opened in 1970.

In the right foreground is the warehouse belonging to Hugh Fox. The gardens and lawn surrounding Sir Thomas Browne's statue have now been removed and the area was paved and landscaped in 1972.

(See Volume One, pages 5 and 6 for details about St. Peter Mancroft Church).

THEATRE STREET, c. 1916

Looking towards Rampant Horse Street and showing St. Stephen's Church on the right, the only building which has survived to this day.

The church, built in the 14th century, had its chancel built in 1501–22 with further additions built in Perpendicular style after the Reformation. The tower, also 14th century, was remodelled in 1601 (notice the date over the door — the date later removed in 1960). The church interior contains an impressive hammer-beam roof, many monuments and brasses. Much of the stained glass is modern, the original glass blown out during World War 2.

Further down in Rampant Horse Street were many late Georgian houses. The Tudor house, which stood at 4–8, Theatre Street and seen in the centre of the picture, was destroyed during the war.

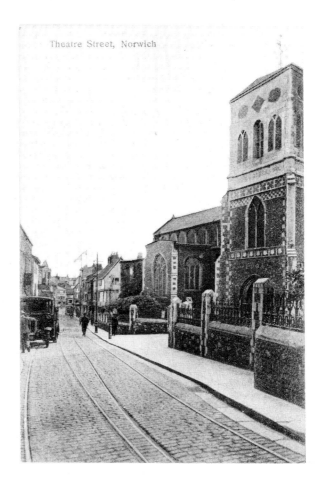

Theatre Street, Norwich

THE THEATRE ROYAL, 1934

A scarce postcard showing the fire which destroyed the second Theatre Royal on 22nd June, 1934.
The fire started near the stage when an assistant noticed flames coming from under the safety curtain. The Fire Brigade were called immediately, but within two hours, the theatre had suffered extensive damage. The new theatre, the third built on the site, was opened on 30th September, 1935. During the Norwich Blitz, two incendiary bombs dropped on the theatre roof but were quickly extinguished. The theatre was refurbished and modernized in 1971.
On the left of the picture is the spire of St. Peter Mancroft Church and the Trinity Presbyterian Church, the latter badly damaged by fire during the Blitz. The Norwich Central Library now stands on this site.
(For further details about the Theatre Royal see Volume One, page 12.)

THE HIPPODROME, ST. GILES' STREET, 1909

Showing the Hippodrome decorated for the Royal visit to Norwich by H.M. King Edward VII on 25th October, 1909. The theatre, originally known as the Grand Opera House, was renamed the Hippodrome in 1904. It presented many excellent variety shows, and among the famous stars who appeared at the theatre were: Gracie Fields, Laurel and Hardy, Tommy Handley, Max Miller and Hughie Green.

At the time of this photograph, theatre prices at the Hippodrome were: Balcony – 9d; Stalls – 1/-;Dress Circle 1/6d.

The Hippodrome closed in 1960 and demolished in 1966 to make way for a multi-storey car park.

43 NORWICH. — Norwich and London Accident Assurance Cº. — LL.

43, ST. GILES' STREET

This magnificent building, housing the offices of the Norwich and London Accident Assurance Co. Ltd., was designed in Baroque style by G. Skipper and built in 1906.

The outer appearance of the building remains the same today, but it is now occupied by the offices of British Telecom.

ST. GILES' STREET

The western end of St. Giles' Street — looking towards St. Giles-on-the-Hill and, in the centre background, the tower of St. John the Baptist Roman Catholic Church.

The number 23 tram, on its way to the city centre from Unthank Road, appears to be on a collision course with the motor-car emerging from Willow Lane! Opposite the car, is the entrance to Rigby's Court which leads to Bethel Street. This view is much the same today apart from the removal of the tram lines and overhead wires.

CHAPELFIELD GARDENS, c. 1912

A delightful watercolour, one of a set of six postcards, published by Jarrolds and reproduced as an oil facsimile. This effect was created by brushing the card with varnish, which resulted in the surface of the postcard having the texture of brush-marked oil paint.

The artist, Walter Haywood-Young, who also used the pseudonym "Jotter" for his signature, was born near Sheffield in 1868. His talent was spotted in 1899 by the postcard publishers, Raphael Tuck, who commissioned him to paint watercolour scenes throughout the British Isles. His paintings reproduced on postcards became extremely popular and he was engaged by numerous major publishers. Characteristic of his views was the inclusion of a few human figures, who brought life to his colourful scenes. He died prematurely in 1920 at the age of 51.

ST. STEPHEN'S ROAD, c. 1933

A rare postcard showing the shop and tea rooms of F.& S. Spurgeon at 33–35, St. Stephen's Road. The premises were next to the Norfolk and Norwich Hospital on the left-hand side of the road going towards the city.

Notice the large display boards advertising "Certified milk from Woodton Hall Model Dairy" and "Milk that is safe, pure and clean".

Number 35, St. Stephen's Road was later a confectionery shop.

ST. STEPHEN'S ROAD, p.u. 1905

Looking towards the junctions with Chapel Field Road and Queen's Road. Beyond the horse and cart is the beginning of St. Stephen's Street.

On the extreme left is an advertisement for W. Read, Cab Proprietor, who had landaus and wagonettes for hire. Among the businesses which occupied the row of buildings were: No. 15 – a chemist (notice the sign above the blind); No. 9 – The Coachmakers' Arms public house. The entrance to the coachyard can be seen by the lamp-post. At a later date, Morgan's Brewery replaced the roadside pub-sign (shown on the postcard) by a new sign, affixed to the front of the building. The new sign weighs nearly a ton and shows the old St. Stephen's Gate.

ST. STEPHEN'S GATE

The city walls were first built in the 12th century and rebuilt over fifty years between 1294 and 1343. The walls, 20 feet high and 2¼ miles in length, surrounded the city except on its eastern flank where the city is protected by the River Wensum.

St. Stephen's Gate was one of twelve gates which guarded and allowed access to the inner city. The other gates were St. Benedict's, St. Giles', Ber Street, Brazen, Conesford (King Street), Bishopgate, Pockthorpe, Magdalen, St. Augustine's, St.Martin-at-Oak and Heigham.

The gates were demolished in the late eighteenth century in c. 1792.

The postcard was one of a set of twenty cards published by Jarrolds illustrating ten of the city gates. The cards were printed from the original engravings of Henry Ninham made in 1864, which had been based on drawings made by H. Kirkpatrick in 1720.

J. KIRKPATRICK, 1720.   H. NINHAM 1864

ST. STEPHEN'S GATE.
(OUTSIDE)

VICTORIA GOODS STATION c. 1920
A photograph of the Great Eastern Railway Goods Team standing in front of the stables, near the weighbridge and main gate at Victoria Goods Station.
Two people have been identified: Jack Coates (horse loader) and Teddy Jolly.
(For further details about Victoria Station see Volume One, page 34.)

GROVE ROAD, p.u. 1916

Looking towards the old railway bridge at Victoria Station; the bridge having been recently demolished.
On the left, the buildings have all disappeared. The Surrey Grove public house was severely damaged during an air raid in April 1942.
On the right is the junction with Southwell Road. The houses and shop, including the post-box, still remain, but the iron railings have been removed.
Notice the postman emptying the post-box and the selection of enamel advertisements above the shop. These would certainly be collector's items today.

CROWE STREET, c. 1910

A fancy-dress parade, part of a street celebration, by the local residents of Rows 13 and 21, Crowe Street; photographed by the Norwich photographer, Tom Nokes.

Crowe Street was on the south side of Southwell Road; Row 13 situated on the north side between numbers 70 and 72, Southwell Road; and Row 21 situated between Southwell Road Garage and Arthur Mansfield's grocery shop.

BER STREET, c. 1912

A.&W. Harl's ironmongery and general store which was situated at 113 Ber Street.
The owner, Mr. A. Harl, stands outside his shop with its fascinating window display which includes: paraffin, table-lamps, frying-pans, tin baths, pails and crockery. Also, notice the advertisements for fireworks.
No doubt when entering the interior, one would have discovered a real life "Aladdin's Cave".

THE N.A.A.F.I. CLUB, c. 1944

Bunting's drapery store, situated on the corner of St. Stephen's and Rampant Horse Streets, was seriously damaged during an air raid in World War 2. The building was converted and became the N.A.A.F.I. Club for off-duty allied service personnel until the end of the war.
After the war, the building was extensively altered to become Marks and Spencer's.

RED LION STREET, c. 1912

Looking towards Orford Hill and Castle Meadow, with a number 16 tram heading in the same direction.
In the left foreground is H.P. Colman's furnishing and ironmongery shop; the building was later destroyed in the Blitz.
On the extreme right is the Coach and Horses public house and at the time of this photograph, the landlord was
Mrs. Mary Alice Seppings. Today the premises are occupied by Pizzaland.

ORFORD PLACE, p.u. 1908

Burlington Buildings, seen in the centre of the picture, were designed in Queen Anne style by the architect, J. Owen Bond, built in 1904, and occupied by various offices.

In the left background is part of St. Peter Mancroft Church and the beginning of Haymarket. In the foreground is the junction with Red Lion Street, and to the right, Orford Hill leading to Castle Meadow. In the centre and right background is the entrance to the Lamb Inn's yard (see Volume One, page 44) and George Smith, flour and corn merchants. The street running immediately in front of the buildings was formerly known as Little Orford Street.

Five trams are visible at the tram terminus, and the correspondent has written a short message on the reverse of the post-card, "Rather busy isn't it?"

Today, this view is obscured following the construction of Debenham's store.

ORFORD PLACE, c. 1925

This view continues on from the previous page, but has been photographed at a later date.
On the left is Thomas Ling, ironmongers, and in the centre, Orford Hill and Castle Meadow, with the Castle beyond. Behind the tram, which is on its way to Trowse, is the Bell Hotel and The Orford Arms public house (now occupied on the corner by the Halifax Building Society). Part of Anchor Buildings can be seen on the right, with A. L. Jones & Co. Ltd., tobacconists, occupying the shop at street level.

THE ROYAL ARCADE, 1911

Photographed looking towards Castle Meadow from Gentleman's Walk, and showing the Royal Arcade decorated for the Coronation celebrations and Royal visit of H.M. King George V in June 1911.

The Royal Arcade, designed by George Skipper and built in 1900, on the site of the former Royal Hotel, remains much the same today. However, a modernisation programme is being carried out at present, with the original shop-fronts being retained.

(See also Volume One, page 47).

YE OLDE LONDON STREETE, NORWICH.

LONDON STREET, 1911

A rare postcard showing the magnificent arch, at the entrance to London Street from Bank Plain, constructed and decorated for the Royal visit of H.M. King George V on 28th June, 1911.
On the left is Nutall and Mason, chemists, and on the right, J.S. Ellison, tobacconist. Through the arch, the businesses identified include: No. 69 – motor clothing manufacturers; No. 67 – the office of the G.W.R. (Eastern Region); and No. 65 – Bowhill and Elliott, military boot and shoe makers.
(See also Volume One, pages 56 and 94.)

REDWELL STREET, c. 1910

Looking down Redwell Street from Bank Plain, with the tram lines leading on down St. Andrew's Street, having merged to form a single track from the passing loop in the foreground.

In the centre is the 15th-century church of St. Michael-at-Plea, which owes its name to the Archdeacon who held his courts there. Sadly, the church has become one of Norwich's redundant churches and is now used as an antique centre and a Sue Ryder coffee shop. Before closing, some wonderful mediæval painted panels were removed and are now displayed in the Cathedral. Notice the 'Forget-me-not' clock on the church tower and the St. Michael and Dragon over the porch.

Other details in the picture include: on the left, the premises of Geo. Bury, furniture dealer, and Charles Payne; in the centre, Princes Street Congregational Church behind St. Michael-at-Plea; and on the right, the junction with Queen Street and part of the factory building belonging to P. Haldinstein & Sons, shoe manufacturers.

THE ROYAL HOTEL

This aerial photograph shows the fine proportions of the Royal Hotel. The photograph was taken by Fred Low, official photographer for the Norfolk and Norwich Aero Club. All of his negatives were destroyed in an air raid on Mousehold Aerodrome on 19th July, 1941.

The view shows Castle Meadow in the left foreground; Bank Plain, top left; Bank Street, behind the Royal Hotel; Upper King Street, top right; Agricultural Hall Plain, in the foreground; and the beginning of Prince of Wales Road in the right foreground.

The postcard was probably used for publicity purposes by the hotel.

AGRICULTURAL HALL ROLLER SKATING RINK & STAFF, NORWICH.

ROLLER-SKATING RINK, AGRICULTURAL HALL, c. 1905

The Agricultural Hall was opened by The Prince of Wales (later H.M. King Edward VII) in 1882. For a time, the building was used as a roller-skating rink.

This postcard, also used for advertising purposes, has the following details printed on the reverse: popular prices – Mondays, Wednesdays and Fridays – 6d admission. 6d for use of skates.

(See also Volume One, pages 52 and 57).

Christmas Eve-
Norwich - P.O.
(Country Road Letters) ③

NORWICH POST OFFICE, c. 1907

A rare postcard showing the interior of the old Head Post Office in Prince of Wales Road on Christmas Eve, with vast piles of letters and cards ready for Christmas Day delivery.

NORWICH CHRISTMAS POSTMARK

One of the scarcest postmarks, to be found on postcards, is the Christmas Cross. This special postmark was applied to letters and cards handed in to the Post Office from 12–22 December, with delivery guaranteed on Christmas Day. Norwich was the only city in East Anglia to use this Postal Delivery Service and was only in operation in 1907 and 1908. (An oval Christmas Cross was allocated for 1903, but to the author's knowledge, one has never been seen). This type of postmark was more widely used in the Liverpool and Manchester areas between 1902 and 1909.

The message "Is this a Christmas or a New Year's card?" refers to the fact that the front of the card is a date card for 1908.

PRINCE OF WALES ROAD, c. 1937

Looking up Prince of Wales Road towards the Shire Hall, the Boer War Memorial and Castle Meadow.
On the left is Mann Egerton's motor-car showrooms, and beyond, the old Head Post Office. On the right, next to the Royal Hotel, are: City Chambers Insurance Offices; The Prince of Wales public house; F.W. Snelling, tobacconist; Lanham & Co, florist; and on the extreme right, J. Langley & Co. Ltd. – Toyland. Adjacent to the number 80 bus, on its way to Harvey Lane, is Lanham's delivery van.
(For a close-up of F.W. Snelling's shop; see Volume One, page 58)

TOMBLAND, c. 1925

Tombland, originally a Saxon market place and the site of the City's fairs until 1818, is bordered by many historic buildings.

This more unusual postcard view shows part of the west side of Tombland. From left to right the buildings are: Plowright's antiques shop; the Central Hotel; solicitor's and barristers' offices; the church of St. George Tombland at the entrance to Prince's Street; and the Army and Navy Stores public house, formerly the Tombland Stores public house which opened in 1870, and today renamed the 'Edith Cavell'.

The 15th-century church of St. George Tombland contains some fine and interesting feaures including: a 17th-century font cover; and an 18th-century pulpit and reredos.

TOMBLAND, c. 1930

An attractive postcard showing part of the east side of Tombland.
On the right is St. Ethelbert's House built in 1888. At the time of this photograph, the building was occupied by an antique shop. Today, it is occupied by Boswell's Restaurant.
Notice the furniture displayed outside the shop, and only three parked cars!

S 1457   HERCULES HOUSE. NORWICH.

SAMSON AND HERCULES HOUSE, c. 1922

The four-gabled Samson and Hercules House, named after the curious statues supporting the porch, was built in 1657 on the site of an earlier 15th-century house owned by the Duchess of Suffolk. The two statues (one of which is a modern replacement) used to stand in the yard behind the house.

The building has had many uses in the past: a dance hall, well known to off-duty troops in the last war; the Y.M.C.A.; and more recently, Ritzy's night club.

On the left is part of Augustine Steward House, occupied at the time by Cubitt & Sons. To the right of Samson and Hercules House is the beginning of Wensum Street, and the Wagon and Horses public house (now the Louis Marchesi public house).

TOMBLAND ALLEY, c. 1922

Tombland Alley, a quaint stone-paved and cobbled passageway skirting the church-yard of St. George Tombland (seen on the left of the picture), links Tombland with Princes Street. Many picturesque old gabled houses can be seen, but the most interesting house, with one of its rooms built over the entrance to the alley, is Augustine Steward's House.

Augustine Steward, a wealthy merchant, was deputy Mayor of the City at the time of Kett's Rebellion in 1549. The house being used as the headquarters of the two Royal armies sent to suppress the rebellion. The building is particularly noted for its fine oak panelling.

At the time of this photograph, the house was occupied by Cubitt & Sons, antique furniture dealers. In more recent years it housed the Norwich Tourist Information Centre, and today, is occupied by the Corbus Restaurant.

NORWICH. — The Grammar School. — LL.

THE GRAMMAR SCHOOL, p.u. 1912

Passing through the Erpingham Gate and entering the Upper Close, the Grammar School stands to the west of the Cathedral.

The postcard shows the chapel built in 1316 by Bishop Salmon. It was later used as a charnel-house (bone depository) until 1548, and in 1550, it was purchased by the City to house the free Grammar School already established by King Edward VI.

After World War 1, the chapel ceased to be used for teaching purposes and was rededicated as the school chapel; the scholars moving into the adjacent School House.

The school has had several notable scholars including: Horatio Nelson; Edward Coke, Chief Justice of England; James Brooke, later Rajah of Sarawak; and George Borrow, author.

THE CLOSE, c. 1910

One of the "Quaint Old Norwich" series of postcards, showing some of the gabled houses which line Hook's Walk — a delightful narrow street connecting Bishopgate with Lower Close.

Of particular interest, and shown in the centre of the postcard, is the house at 50, Hook's Walk which was built in 1661 and the former residence of Dr. Frank Sayers, poet, metaphysician and antiquary, between 1792 until his death in 1817. Among his distinguished friends were Sir Walter Scott and the poet Southey, who often met him at his home in Hook's Walk. After his death, the Cathedral library received his fine collection of books.

Quaint Old Norwich.
In the Close

Quaint Old Norwich,
View from Quayside

BECKWITH COURT, c. 1910

Beckwith Court was named after James Christmas Beckwith (1750–1809), organist of Norwich Cathedral and St. Peter Mancroft Church.

Viewed from Quayside, Beckwith Court no longer exists. It was originally located just past the buildings which occupy the Quayside Antiques Centre today.

ELM HILL

Looking towards Blackfriars Hall and the Briton's Arms — formerly a tavern with parts of the building dating back to the fourteenth century. It is now occupied by a coffee house.

On the extreme left is part of Elm Hill Stamp Shop, and in the left background, the famous elm tree — replaced by a London plane tree in 1986, after becoming infected with Dutch elm disease.

Notice the cobbled roadway which still exists today.

Elm Hill showing "Briton Arms," Norwich

37

ST. PETER HUNGATE CHURCH, c. 1938

St. Peter Hungate Church standing in Princes Street, was built on the site of an earlier church by John and Margaret Paston in 1460. The church became redundant in 1933 and is maintained by the City Corporation as a Museum of Ecclesiastical Art. The exhibits include illuminated manuscripts, carvings, paintings and curiosities from churches all over Norfolk.

St. Peter Hungate was the first of several Norwich churches to be put to an alternative use.

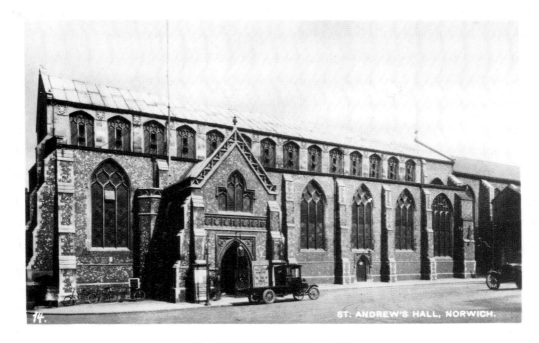

ST. ANDREW'S HALL, c. 1920

St. Andrew's Hall was once the nave of the Dominican or Black Friars church of Norwich, built in 1440 and completed in 1470.

On the right of the picture is part of Blackfriars Hall, which was originally the chancel to the church. An octagonal tower used to stand above the centre of the building, but it collapsed in 1712.

After the Reformation, the church was purchased in 1540 by Augustine Steward on behalf of the City Corporation. The building was restored in 1863 by T.D. Barry, the City Surveyor.

The halls are used for a great variety of events, including concerts, meetings, exhibitions and antique and craft fairs.

THEATRE DE LUXE, ST. ANDREW'S STREET, c. 1920's

An early advertising postcard showing the interior of the Theatre de Luxe, the first Norwich cinema.

The original building, which stood between the junctions of Bridewell Alley and Exchange Street, was erected as the Royal Bazaar in 1831. Later it served as the Norwich Technical Institute and then converted to the Theatre de Luxe, which opened on 9th April 1910. It introduced sound pictures in 1931. Sadly, the cinema closed in 1959 and the building was demolished in 1971.

How many readers remember sitting in the back row?

THE BRIDEWELL MUSEUM, c. 1923

The original building, a private house, was built in c. 1370 by the father of William Appleyard, the first Mayor of Norwich. It became the Brydewell (Bridewell), or prison, for vagrants in 1583. Most of the building was destroyed by fire in 1751, but it was rebuilt and remained a prison until 1828, when the inmates were transferred to a new prison outside St. Giles' Gates.

Since then, the building has been a tobacco factory, leather warehouse, and in 1896, it became Thomas Bowhill's boot and shoe factory which moved to Heigham Street in 1923. The building was donated to the city the same year, and opened on 24th October, 1925 by the Duke of York as a museum of local industries, trades and crafts.

The postcard shows the splendid knapped-flint wall overlooking St. Andrew's Churchyard.

THE MADDERMARKET THEATRE

The Maddermarket Theatre is one of the celebrated repertory theatres in Britain, and the home of the Norwich Players founded by Walter Nugent Monk in 1911.

The theatre occupies a building erected in 1794 as a Roman Catholic Church. Later, it became a Salvation Army Hall, and a warehouse. After World War 1, Nugent Monk and the Norwich Players converted the building into a reconstruction of a Shakespearian theatre, which opened in 1921. An extension was made to the theatre in 1966.

The Maddermarket Theatre is located off St. John's Alley, after passing through an arch under the tower of St. John Maddermarket Church.

ST. BENEDICT'S STREET, c. 1912

St. Benedict's Street is one of the oldest inhabited areas of the city. In the last century, it was no more than a muddy street, but the area was so densely populated that it required four churches. Three of these churches, St. Swithin's, St. Margaret's and St. Lawrence, have become redundant and are now converted to alternative use.

This view shows the western end of St. Benedict's Street and looks towards St. Benedict's Gate and the beginning of Dereham Road. On the left, the buildings include: No. 106 – The White Lion public house; and beyond the junction with Duck Lane (now Wellington Lane), No. 112 – H.E. Baldwin, milliner and fancy draper. On the right of the picture, the buildings include (left to right): No. 89 – The Fountain public house, an old coaching inn (the white building beyond the horse and cart); Nos. 87 – 79. For details about the occupancy of these premises and a view of the opposite direction of St. Benedict's, see Volume One, page 89.

ST. MARY AT COSLANY, ST. MARY PLAIN, 1908

The church was built in Perpendicular style on the site of an earlier church. The building joined an Anglo-Saxon round flint tower, which has survived to this day.

The church closed in 1892 and re-opened after restoration costing £2,200 in 1909. The postcard showing repair work to the flint walls and tower photographed in 1908. Further restoration was necessary after World War 2, following a serious fire which damaged the church roof.

Today, St. Mary at Coslany is under the control of the Norwich Historic Churches Trust and is now used as a craft centre.

BARNARDS LTD., COSLANY STREET, c. 1930

Barnard, Bishop and Barnard's Norfolk Iron Works were founded in 1855.
The foundry, later to be known as Barnards Ltd., manufactured brass, ironwork, kitchen stoves and wire-netting. It occupied about an acre of land to the east of Coslany Street and to the north of the river between St. Miles and Duke's Palace Bridges. The site is now occupied by a modern housing development built in the 1970s.
The postcard shows a selection of Barnard's products displayed at a local trade show; the exact date and location are unknown.

OLD NORWICH, VIEW FROM RIVER.

No. 1847

RIVER VIEW FROM ST. GEORGE'S BRIDGE, p.u. 1904

Photographed from St. George's Bridge and showing, on the left, two wherries unloading their cargoes of timber, brought upriver from Yarmouth, at the timber merchant's yard belonging to James Porter. On the right is the wherry "Sagamore" (26 tons, 54ft. long and 15ft. beam) unloading at Blackfriars Wharf near the yard belonging to John W. Lacey, slate, tile and brick merchants. Blackfriars Wharf is now the site of the Art School erected by the Norwich Corporation in 1899.

St. George's Bridge (also known as Black-friars Bridge) was built in 1784 on the site of an earlier mediæval bridge. It was designed by Sir John Soane and constructed as a single-span bridge in Portland stone.

COLEGATE, c. 1916

Showing the former Martineau Memorial Hall and Sunday School, designed by H. Chatfield Clarke and built in 1907. The building is now occupied by a carpet centre. It was named after Harriet Martineau, the authoress, and her brother James, the Unitarian theologian, who had their early home at 10, Magdalen Street.

Just out of view on the left, and behind the main gates shown in the centre, is the Octagon Chapel, built for the Presbyterians in 1754–6 by Thomas Ivory, the Norwich architect. After 1820 it was used by the Unitarians.

In the right background is the junction with Magdalen Street to the left and Fye Bridge Street to the right. Also on the right and out of view is St. Clement's Church.

ANGUISH'S SCHOOL, FISHERGATE, c. 1906

Anguish's School, or more popularly known as "Blue Coat" or "Bluebottle" School because of it's uniform, was founded by Thomas Anguish (Mayor of Norwich 1611) in 1621 for the proper education of poor children.

The distinctive uniform consisted of a flat red woollen cap with blue band, and blue woollen top knot; a black speckled scarlet waistcoat; and a short blue cut-away coat with brass buttons.

The school was situated on the north side of Fishergate, halfway between the junctions with Peacock (now Blackfriars) Street and the lower half of Cowgate Street (now Whitefriars). The school building in Fishergate closed in 1885, later becoming part of Sexton's shoe works, and in the mid-1930s the schoolhouse was demolished to allow the road to be widened.

MAGDALEN STREET, p.u. 1915

Looking north towards Magdalen Gates and the junction with Magpie Road and Bull Close Road. Magdalen Street is one of the oldest thoroughfares in the city and the main shopping centre north of the river.

On the left is the shop for the sale of goods manufactured by the Norwich Institution for the Blind, founded by Thomas Tawell, a wealthy local merchant, in 1805. The buildings were demolished during the Anglia Square development and the Institution moved to Thomas Tawell House, off Magpie Road.

In the centre, the tall building is the Jolly Brewers public house (No. 134), and in the right foreground, the barber's pole belongs to the hairdresser, F. Garner. (See also Volume 1, page 73).

MAGDALEN ROAD, c. 1928

Showing the former Artichoke public house owned by Youngs, Crawshay and Youngs, on its corner site at the junction with Bull Close Road. At the time the licensee was Fred Sinclair.

Previously, this 15th-century building was occupied in turn by a leper house, almshouse, and a workhouse, before it became an alehouse. The present "Artichoke" was built in 1932 with its round bays reminiscent of the city gates.

SEWELL PARK, p.u. 1912

Photographed at the junction of St. Clement's Hill and Constitution Hill and showing the entrance to Sewell Park. In the foreground, the horse trough has the inscription — "Erected by N. & N. Branch of the R.S.P.C.A. 1908".
In the right foreground, the tram lines lead from Denmark Road, on the right, towards the beginning of Magdalen Road.

LAZAR HOUSE, 219 SPROWSTON ROAD, p.u. 1907

The Lazar Hospital was founded by Bishop Herbert de Losinga at the beginning of the 12th century, and was known locally as the Magdalen Chapel. The building is situated close to the junction of Gilman Road with Sprowston Road. It was restored in 1907 by Sir Eustace Gurney J.P., who presented it to the city in 1921. Since this date, Lazar House has been used as a branch library.

SPROWSTON MILL, c. 1920

Sprowston Mill, built in 1730 on Mousehold Heath, was an early post-mill; the mill turning on a central post with the wind. It was destroyed by fire on 23rd March, 1933, just before restoration work was due to be carried out.

The mill became known as "Old Crome's Mill" after it had been featured in the well-known painting "A Mill on the Heath" by the artist and founder of the Norwich School of Painting, John Crome (1768–1821).

SPROWSTON HALL, NORWICH.

SPROWSTON HALL, p.u. 1913

Sprowston Hall was built in c. 1559. Situated close to the Wroxham Road, the hall was rebuilt in 1881, and for many years it was the home of Sir Eustace Gurney, J.P..

After World War 2, the hall became the Sprowston Manor Hotel. Today, the 40-bedroom hotel provides a popular venue for weddings and a wide variety of business functions, including conferences, trade shows and antique fairs.

NORTH WALSHAM ROAD, OLD CATTON, c. 1912

Looking north-east along North Walsham road and photographed at the junction of Constitution Hill, in the foreground, with George Hill on the left and School Lane on the right — a quiet rural scene compared with the busy road junction of today.

On the left, the blacksmith's forge has been replaced by a butcher's shop, and the white building, on the other side of the junction with George Hill, is now a car park for The Woodman public house. On the right, the row of cottages still remain and beyond, the village grocery shop stands on the corner with School Lane.

OLD CATTON MURDER, p.u. 1908

Several postcards were published recording the events in connection with the murder of nineteen-year-old Eleanor (Nellie) Howard by Horace Larter, her boyfriend, of Ber Stret, Norwich.
This postcard shows the crowds outside the Maid's Head Inn, Spixworth Road, Old Catton, where the murder inquest was held on 2nd November, 1908. The jury later returned a verdict of wilful murder.

PELHAM ROAD, NEW CATTON, c. 1912

Pelham Road runs from Millers Lane to St. Clement's Hill.
The postcard shows the corner grocery shop, owned at the time by Mr. J. Love, which stood on the corner of Pelham and Norman Roads. The enamel signs on the wall advertise Brasso, Gossage's soap, Swift polish and Fry's chocolate.
One of the many window advertisements reads: "Mary had a little lamb with lots of H.P. sauce today".

ST. AUGUSTINE'S STREET, c. 1912

Looking north-west down St. Augustine's Street, photographed near the junction with Pitt Street and Botolph Street, with St. Augustine's churchyard on the left.

St. Augustine's Church, out of view, was built in Decorated and Perpendicular styles on the site of an earlier church in 1726.

The premises on the right include: The Rose Inn; the entrance to Rose Yard (see page 59); and No. 3 – Dawson's drapery shop.

The street appears to have plenty of activity with pony and traps and hand carts in view.

ROSE YARD, c. 1910

Rose Yard is one of several yards which back on to Augustine's Street. At the time of this photograph, which looks towards St. Augustine's Church, the entrance to Rose Yard was at the side of Rose Tavern (now occupied by a shop). Access is still possible from St. Augustine's Street and today, there is also a footpath to Rose Yard from Edward Street. Notice the dress of the people posed for the photograph, the gas lamps and the small shop on the right, which sold everything from lamp oil, Lambert's tea and Hudson's soap. The advertising signs on the wall would certainly be collector's items today.

ST. AUGUSTINE'S STREET

Published by Wood & Co of Fye Bridge, this postcard shows a continuation of St. Augustine's Street, photographed near the junction with Esdelle Street.

The Catherine Wheel public house can be seen on the right-hand side of the street, in the centre of the picture. Also on the right, are A. W. Hall, stonemason, and in the foreground, Brock Bros., tailors, hatters and breeches maker.

Notice the advertising sign on one of the first-floor windows: "Trousers to measure – 10/6d per pair".

(See also Volume 1, page 82 for a view of the left-hand side of St. Augustine's Street).

54, ST. AUGUSTINE'S STREET, c. 1908

A rare postcard showing St. Augustine's Cash Boot Stores with the proprietor, Mr. A. F. Neave, standing in the doorway. The advertising in the window reads: "Bespoke Work". The prices of the boots and shoes range from 3/3d, 4/11d, 6/11d and 7/6d.

SUSSEX STREET, c. 1928

An advertising postcard produced for Bush & Twiddy, motor body-builders, Croft Works, Sussex Street. The photograph shows before and after views of a vehicle, registration number CL 4052, converted to a twelve-seater open-top charabanc with its collapsible rain hood at the rear.

Bush & Twiddy Sussex St. Norwich

AYLSHAM ROAD, p.u. 1914

Looking towards the city and photographed near the junctions of Patteson and Drayton Roads. The houses on the left have seen little change over the years, and a No. 12 tram can be seen passing the junction with Buxton Road. In the right background is the spire of St. Augustine's School, now the site of the Norwich Swimming Baths. (See also Volume 1, page 83).

BERNERS STREET, p.u. 1912
Photographed from Vicarage Road across Aylsham Road and showing the entrance to Berners Street.
On the right can be seen George Towell's corner shop and sub-post office, with many wall advertisements including
Rowntree's cocoa and chocolate. Today, there is still a corner shop but no post office.
(See also Volume 1, page 85).

NORWICH SPEEDWAY TEAM, c. 1946

The Norwich Speedway team photographed at the Firs Speedway Stadium, Cromer Road, opposite The Firs public house. The stadium is now a housing estate.

At the time, the speedway team, known as "The Stars", were:- Back row, left to right – Paddy Mills, Ted Bravery, Bert Spencer, Roy Duke, Wilf Jay, and Don Houghton. Front row, left to right – Len Read, Dick Wise (Manager), and Sid Hipperson.

HELLESDON STATION, c. 1912

Hellesdon Station was opened by the Midland and Great Northern Railway at the end of the 19th century. It was the first station after leaving City Station on the journey to Melton Constable, and its design was typical of M. & G.N. station buildings with its two gable ends. It possessed a single platform, goods sidings, but no passing loop. The station eventually closed to passengers in 1953.

Today, the adjacent railway line is now a seven-mile nature walk to Attlebridge, known as Marriott's Way; named after William Marriott, chief engineer to the Midland and Great Northern Railway Company.

THE "RED LION", DRAYTON, p.u. 1935

The Red Lion public house situated at Drayton crossroads has changed little over the years and looks very similar today.
At the time of the photograph, the proprietor was Mr. C. W. Neve.
A splendid tourer, registration number PW 7190, is parked outside the "Red Lion" and a double-decker bus, NG 2733, is ready for its return to the city centre.

HEIGHAM GROVE, NORWICH.

HEIGHAM GROVE, c. 1925

Heigham Grove lies between Mill Hill Road and Chester Place on the southern side of Earlham Road.
The street remains much the same today, with the exception of the house with the stone portico, shown in the right foreground, which has been replaced by modern flats.
The postcard was published by a local stationer, Harold Palmer, of 55 Earlham Road.

SWAN BATHS, HEIGHAM STREET, p.u. 1907

The Swan Laundry and Swan Baths, the city's first indoor pool, were built in 1879; steam from the laundry being used to heat the pool. A year after the pool was built, a group of swimmers formed the Swan Swimming Club which continued to use the pool until it closed in 1933.

In the early 1900s and possibly before, swimming races were held in the river with many spectators lining the banks. On one such occasion, it was reported that one of the swimmers swallowed a portion of a dead rat whilst competing and was immediately taken to hospital. The outcome of this unpleasant accident is unknown!

The postcard view of the Swan Baths shows the caretaker's house on the left, and the changing rooms beside the River Wensum. Today, this site is occupied by Herrells (Norwich) Ltd., steel stockholders.

NORWICH SWAN SWIMMING CLUB, c. 1920s

This photograph was taken at one of the gaia-days held at the Swan Baths. Guests of honour at these galas had to be provided with some form of protection or their clothes would become saturated by the splashes from the swimmers and divers. Notice the spectators looking up at one of the divers — part of the legs just visible on the upper diving board. The Swan Swimming Club is still in existence today, using St. Augustine's Baths and various school baths for training.

DIAL SQUARE, c. 1920

Dial Square is located on the corner of Mile Cross Road and Heigham Street, with Heigham Watering to the rear. The houses on the left have been demolished, so the large house now faces Mile Cross Road. The sundial has been removed and has been repositioned above the circular name plaque which is now blank. These buildings are semi-derelict at present.

HEIGHAM STREET, p.u. 1910

Looking towards the city centre and photographed at the junction with Old Palace Road, showing the entrance to Home Street on the left and various shops on both sides of the road. Notice the rough surface of the road, and the road sign 'Old Palace Road' at the top of the gas lamp.
Today, this scene has changed beyond all recognition. the area has been completely redeveloped with a garage on the left, modern housing on the right, and a wider road.

ERECTING NEW BRIDGE, HEIGHAM FERRY, NORWICH, MARCH 31st 1909
(PIONEER SERIES)

HEIGHAM BRIDGE (1), p.u. 1909

A photograph, published as a postcard, showing the construction of Heigham Bridge by D.G. Somerville, structural engineers, in March 1909. The new bridge over the River Wensum replaced the old Heigham Ferry and connected a footpath from the back of the Dolphin Inn with another footpath leading to Drayton Road.

HEIGHAM BRIDGE (2), c.1910

The completed Heigham Bridge was opened by the Lord Mayor of Norwich on 16th December, 1909. The bridge is still in use today.

New Bridge, Heigham — Norwich. — Pioneer Series.

HEIGHAM BRIDGE (3), c. 1910

This view shows the continuation of the bridge which crossed the Midland and Great Northern Railway line from the City Station to Melton Constable. Notice the smoke stains on the bridge.
The footbridge is still in use today, but the railway line is now a footpath.

20 NORWICH. — *The Dolphin Inn.* — LL. *1915*

THE DOLPHIN INN

The Dolphin Inn has a fascinating history going back nearly four hundred years. It was originally built at the end of the 16th century by Richard Browne, a former sheriff of Norwich. The gable end, shown on the left, is dated 1595, and the section with the bay windows is dated 1615. It became known as the Bishop's Palace after Bishop Hall who had taken residence, after he had been forced to leave his palace during the Civil War.

Later the building became the Dolphin Inn. At the time when this postcard was published, the 'Dolphin' was a Steward and Patterson's public house. During one of the 1942 air raids, the building was badly damaged by fire. It was rebuilt in 1960 with the ancient flint frontage carefully restored, and is still a public house today.

13A, DEREHAM ROAD, c. 1912

Mr. John Dodson, grocer and tea dealer, with his assitant standing outside his shop; not far from the junction with Barn Road, on the right-hand side of Dereham Road when leaving the city.

The splendid window displays feature tinned goods of pilchards, salmon and crayfish. By 1925, the grocery business changed to The International Tea Company Ltd.

(See also Volume 1, page 88, which shows an approximate location of John Dodson's shop in the centre background).

DEREHAM ROAD, p.u. 1923

Photographed close to Adelaide Street and looking in a westerly direction along Dereham Road. The tram is approaching the junction with St. Philip's Road on the left, and the two ladies are not far from the junction of Nelson Street. What ever happened to the wooden public telephone box on the right?

DEREHAM ROAD SUNDAY SCHOOL OUTING, c. 1910

A very rare postcard showing the Dereham Road Primitive Methodist Sunday Schools' outing ready to depart. The location and destination are unknown, but the photograph must have been taken close to Norwich. The carts, borrowed from various firms, have candle lamps, and the cycles have carbide lamps.
This remarkable record of social history shows the changes that have taken place in travel and entertainment over the last eighty years. Can you imagine a similar spectacle today?

BOWTHORPE ROAD, c. 1914

Looking towards Dereham Road and showing The Union; later named the Norwich Public Assistance Institution, or more commonly known as the Workhouse. On the opposite side of the road, and out of view, was the Isolation Hospital. Today, the buildings beside the road have been demolished and The Union is now the site of the West Norwich Hospital.

CENTRAL STORES, THE STREET, COSSEY, c. 1912

For many years, the Central Stores were owned by Mr. E. F. Ottaway, grocer and baker, of Cossey (now spelt Costessey). Notice the left-hand window display with the pyramid of tinned goods, and also the advertisement in the right-hand window — "Eiffel Tower Lemonade: 2 gallons – 4d". In the left foreground, the baker's delivery-cart is full of unwrapped and unprotected freshly-baked loaves of bread; their tempting aroma certain to attract many customers.

The buildings remain much the same today, but the grocery shop is now occupied by a hairdressing salon.

EARLHAM HALL, c. 1924

Earlham Hall stands within the extensive grounds of Earlham Park, east of the River Yare. The Hall has a variety of architectural styles: the west front is dated 1642; the south front is late-17th century; the north front, 17th century and Georgian; and the one-storeyed pavilion — shown in the left foreground — is probably of Georgian origin.

The Hall was built by Robert Houghton and passed through different owners until the Norwich City Council purchased the 356-acre Earlham Hall Estate in 1925. The most famous occupants, who never actually owned the house, were the Gurney family, the great Quaker bankers and philanthropists, who lived there from 1786 to 1895, including Elizabeth Gurney, one of seven sisters, later to become Elizabeth Fry, the great prison reformer.

Earlham Hall is now part of the University of East Anglia which opened during the early 1960s.

NORWICH MULTI-VIEW POSTCARD, c. 1913

A multi-view postcard showing eleven views in the Newmarket Road area, south-east of the city centre.
The views, which can all be found on separate postcards, include Melrose Road, Waldeck Road, Unthank Road,
Christchurch, Eaton, The Jenny Lind Hospital (see Volume 1, pages 21 and 22), and Cringleford Mill (see Volume 1,
page 105).

THE JENNY LIND HOSPITAL, 1929

The foundation stone of the Out-Patients' Department was laid in 1928 by Mrs. Raymond Maude, daughter of the singer Jenny Lind, after whom the hospital was named.

The building was designed by Edward Boardman, and the postcard shows the opening ceremony for the new Out-Patients' Department by H.R.H. Princess Mary, Viscountess Lascelles, on 29th June, 1929.

Among the civic dignitaries on the dias are: the Bishop of Norwich, the Lord Mayor of Norwich, the Town Clerk, the Sheriff, Mr. Russell Colman, and Mr. G. E. Woolsey, chairman of the Management Committee.

After the ceremony, Princess Mary went on to open Woodrow Pilling Park at Thorpe.

Unthank Road, Norwich.

UNTHANK ROAD, p.u. 1909

Looking towards the city centre with the junction of Cambridge Street visible in the background on the right.
Tram-car, number 1, on the Unthank Road to Riverside Road route, is about to enter the passing loop on its journey.
The houses on the right of the picture still stand today.

TOM NOKES, CHESTER STREET, 1911

Tom Nokes of 9 Chester Street, Norwich, was a well-known prolific photographer, who specialised in portraiture, weddings and landscape photography. He is best remembered for his outstanding animal and rural scenes, many of which were taken in the towns and villages to the south of Norwich, Ashwellthorpe, Hethersett, Mulbarton, Swardeston and Wymondham, travelling by train with his bicycle and then cycling round the countryside taking his photographs.

Examples of his work are keenly sought after by local postcard collectors. (Notice the sheep-drawn cart — lower left).

NORFOLK AND NORWICH HOSPITAL, p.u. 1909

Photographed at a local trade show and showing an exhibition model of a ward at the Norfolk and Norwich Hospital. The "patient" on his crutches adds reality to the display.

Notice the signs reading: "Funds urgently needed". Eighty years on nothing changes!

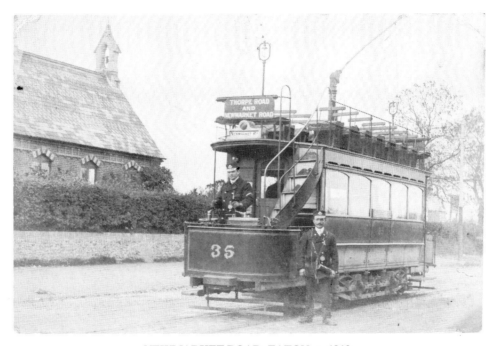

NEWMARKET ROAD, EATON, c. 1912

A rare and very collectable postcard of tram-car, number 35, photographed at the tram terminus on Newmarket Road. The driver and conductor pose for the camera before the tram returns to Thorpe Road.
On the left, on the corner of Unthank Road, the school opened in 1870 and closed in 1928. The building was later demolished.

IPSWICH ROAD, p.u. 1914

The King of Prussia public house, the name visible on the pub sign, at the junction of Ipswich and Hall Roads. Later, this junction was closed, and Hall Road was diverted above the railway bridge, seen on the left, to a new junction below the Post House Hotel.
The name of the public house was changed from "The King of Prussia" to "The King George" during the First World War for patriotic reasons.

CARLYLE ROAD, LAKENHAM, c. 1912

Carlyle Road Post Office stood on the corner of Carlyle and Cricket Ground Roads, not far from the junction with City Road. This typical corner shop sold a wide variety of goods, including wallpapers, saucepans, kettles, canary seed and the usual groceries. Notice the window advertisement for tea – 1/6d, and the enamel sign for Caley's, the local chocolate manufacturer (see also page 118).
The proprietor stands in the doorway, surrounded by his customers of all ages. Notice also the fashions of the day, and especially the baby in the pram.
Today, the shop premises are occupied by a hairdressing salon.

Trowse Station.

TROWSE STATION, p.u. 1909

Looking towards Thorpe Station from Trowse Railway Bridge, showing the sidings to the left and the large cattle pens for stock to and from Norwich market on the right.

Trowse Station opened as a cattle station for the Great Eastern Railway in 1904. The station closed to passenger traffic on 5th September, 1939, and the old iron footbridge with its sheltered walkway and fretwork design was pulled down shortly afterwards — probably to be melted down for the war effort.

After the war, and during the time Trowse Station remained a busy cattle and freight depot, the nearby Pineapple public house had the contract for feeding the cattle awaiting transportation.

Recently, during improvements made at Thorpe Station, Trowse re-opened for passengers for a short period in March 1986 and February 1987. The goods yards are still used today for the conveyance of stone aggregates.

THE ROYAL SHOW, TROWSE, 1911

The Royal Agricultural Show held at Crown Point, Trowse, opened on Monday, 26th June, 1911. Held over five days, the high-point of the Royal Show was the visit of H.M. King George V on Wednesday, 28th June. (See also Volume 1, page 94). The Royal Pavilion, shown above, opened to the public on the last two days of the show; the proceeds of the 3d entrance fee being donated to the Norfolk and Norwich Hospital.

THE SHIP INN, 168 KING STREET, c. 1930

The 16th-century Ship Inn, owned by Youngs, Crawshay and Youngs, stood on the west side of King Street. The inn occupied part of a group of buildings known as Ship Row, not far from the Old Music House. The entrance to Ship Yard can be seen on the left, and notice the entrance to the cellar beneath the second window at street level.

The five-gabled row of homes occupying 164–166 King Street — their origins dating back to Elizabethan times — were demolished in 1939. The Ship Inn was purchased by the City Council in 1970 and converted into two houses.

THE SHIP INN, KING STREET, NORWICH.   12895

MORGAN'S BREWERY CO. LTD., King St., NORWICH. This photograph taken 7th Sept., 1942.

MORGAN'S BREWERY, KING STREET, 1942

A wartime photograph showing horse and motor delivery-drays at Morgan's Brewery Stores and Loading Bay in King Street. At least seventeen staff are visible, and notice the blackouts on the headlamps of the lorries. All draught and bottled beer — no kegs in sight!
Morgan's Brewery was later taken over by Steward and Patterson's Brewery, now part of the Watney Group.

94

MORGAN'S BREWERY, c. 1912
An early steam-powered delivery-dray, built by the Yorkshire Steam Wagon Company of Leeds, photographed at King
Street with its load of 108 crates of beer.
Notice the solid-tyred wheels, and no protection for the driver.

THORPE STATION, NORWICH J & S 349

THORPE STATION, p.u. 1934

Thorpe Station was designed for the Great Eastern Railway Company by John Wilson in 1884. It was built in red brick and yellow stone with a distinctive French pavilion roof.

The station officially opened in 1886 and served rail passengers to Ely, Ipswich and London. It is now the city's only railway station.

Comparing the picture on the front cover of Volume 1, the ornamental gas lamps on the gate posts, and at least two of the gate posts have been removed — possibly to allow easier access to the station forecourt. The postcard above shows the forecourt used as a bus terminus and one of the double-decker buses is advertising Willmott's Radio and Record Shop in Prince of Wales Road. The forecourt is now used as a car park.

ROSARY ROAD, p.u. 1916
The Nest football ground, Rosary Road, the home of Norwich City Football Club from 1908 to 1938, was also used for other entertainments, such as Goodman's Premier Pierrots.
Ticket prices, as advertised on the posters in the background, were 3d, 6d and 1/-; tremendous value for money!

THORPE HAMLET AMBULANCE DEPOT, c. 1941

A very rare wartime postcard photographed at Thorpe Hamlet Ambulance Depot, situated at Thorpe Hamlet School which was near the junction with Ella and St. Leonard's Roads.

The ambulance staff were (left to right): Jimmy Gant, Bert Blower, unknown, Don Landsdel, Mrs. Pledger, Miss Hopkins, Tiger Harvey, Bill Huntingdon, Mrs. Metcalfe, Nobbie Clarke, Joe Coleman, Pop Wilsea, Betty Clarke, Millie Howes, George Cornwall, Bob Howes, Albert Moore, Miss Howsham, Arthur Mouncer, Ted Mison, Harry Norton. No doubt this will evoke wartime memories to some readers and may even prompt a reunion.

KETT'S HILL, c. 1912

Looking up Kett's Hill and showing Mrs. E. Ransome's drapery and haberdashery shop behind the gas lamp; R. A. Elwin, baker, in the centre; and to the right, Kett's Castle public house owned by Youngs, Crawshay and Youngs. These properties have red brick, flint and plastered walls respectively.

Kett's Castle is a reminder of Kett's Rebellion in 1549 when twenty thousand peasant farmers marched on Norwich. Behind the brick wall, in the left foreground, was the depot house for the Barracks. This building later became the vicarage for St. James' Church. The vicarage was demolished in 1938. The brick wall has also been removed and is now the site of a busy roundabout built in 1959.

MOUSEHOLD AERODROME, 1933

Norwich Municipal Airport at Mousehold Aerodrome was opened by H.R.H. The Prince of Wales on 21st June, 1933. The Prince arrived at the airport in a twin-engine De Haviland Dragon, and was welcomed by the Lord Mayor of Norwich, Mr. H. N. Holmes, who was also President of the Norwich Aero Club. After the opening ceremony, the Prince inspected the new clubhouse and the Boulton and Paul Sidestrand bombers of the 101 Squadron. Before his departure, the Prince was presented with a silver cigar box by Capt. A. A. Rice.
Mousehold Aerodrome was situated between the Salhouse and Plumstead Roads, now the Heartsease housing estate.

THORPE VILLAGE, p.u. 1906

Thorpe village lies to the east of the city centre on the A47 Great Yarmouth road.
The postcard view, very familiar to Broads' holidaymakers and photographed from the riverside, shows from left to right:
St. Andrew's Church, The Buck public house, and the post office and village stores, which at the time was owned by Mr. Parker.
St. Andrew's Church was designed by Thomas Jekyll and built of knapped flint, red brick and stone in 1866. It stands beside the ruins of an earlier church. In 1944, a land-mine exploded 1,300 yards from the church, causing a serious crack on the 150ft-high church spire. Ten years later, the spire was replaced by a smaller spire only 30ft. high.
Thorpe village was a popular location for artists of the Norwich School.

THORPE ST. ANDREW HOSPITAL, c. 1916

Patients, nurses, and an ambulance photographed outside St. Andrew's Hospital, which was used as a hospital annexe
during the First World War.
A large number of halls and large homes in Norfolk were used as hospital annexes and convalescent homes for soldiers
wounded in the war.
The oldest part of St. Andrew's dates back to 1811–14, and the hospital is reputed to have been one of the first public
mental hospitals in England.

WHITLINGHAM STATION, p.u. 190

Whitlingham Junction Station opened in 1886 and was situated on the Norwich Thorpe to Yarmouth and Wroxham lines. The junction for the Wroxham line can be seen in the background, leading to the left, past the signal box.
The last ticket was issued by a Mr. Flowers, the duty booking clerk, when the station closed on 18th September, 1955.
The footbridge still remains today.

A VEGETABLE CART

A real gem of social history. A vegetable and flower-seller with his wife photographed somewhere in Norwich. Can any reader identify the location or the two characters?

Notice the now very collectable set of scales in the foreground.

VISIT OF H.M. KING EDWARD VII TO NORWICH (1), 1909

On 25th October, 1909, H.M. King Edward VII departed from Quidenham Hall, where he had been staying with Lord and Lady Albemarle, for a ceremonial visit to Norwich.
The Royal Party, consisting of five cars, travelled via Attleborough, Wymondham and Eaton where the streets had been decorated for the occasion.
The postcard, one of a series illustrating the Royal visit, shows the Royal car (notice the absence of any number plate) heading the procession, and proceeding up Eaton Hill on their way to Norwich. The Cellar House public house can be seen on the left.
(See also Volume 1, page 93).

VISIT OF H.M. KING EDWARD VII TO NORWICH (2), 1909

Over eleven thousand school-children gathered on Mousehold Heath to welcome H.M. King Edward VII. On his arrival, the children sang the National Anthem, which the City authorities had rehearsed the previous day. Later, the children received a bag containing a bun, beef-patty and banana.
Britannia Barracks can be seen in the background.
(See also Volume 1, page 68).

THE PROCLAMATION OF H.M. KING GEORGE V, 1910

Published by Jarrolds and showing the vast crowd assembled in the Market Place, in front of the old Municipal Buildings, to witness the Lord Mayor's Proclamantion of King George V on 9th May, 1910.
Cavalry, foot-soldiers and police stand guard on three sides of the square, and a military band stands in front of the
raised dias for the civic dignitaries and guests of honour.
In the left background is The Royal Exchange public house.

FUNERAL OF SIR GEORGE WHITE MP NORWICH, MAY 15th 1912.

THE FUNERAL OF SIR GEORGE WHITE, 1912

Sir George White was a prominent Norwich citizen and served as a member of parliament for North-West Norfolk at the turn of the century. The George White School in Silver Road, built in 1903, was named after him when he was chairman of the City's Education Committee.

He died, aged 73 years, at Eaton Grange on 11th May, 1912. A private service was held at Eaton Grange on 15th May, the same day as a public memorial service was held at St. Mary's Baptist Church, conducted by Rev. J.H. Shakespeare and Rev. Thomas Phillips. Shops closed and crowds lined the streets to pay their last respects as the funeral procession made its way to the Rosary Cemetery.

The postcard shows the procession passing the Grosvenor Rooms on Prince of Wales Road.

SUFFRAGETTES' MEETING, c. 1912
Three suffragettes standing on a cart, behind the statue of Wellington, addressing a large crowd of onlookers in the
Market Place on a very wet day.
In the background, the buildings are (left to right): Harman and Gowen, accountants; Vandykes, photographers;
Bonser's Stores, tea merchants and grocers; Davey Place; The Jenny Lind public house; and F.R. Underhill, grocers.

NORWICH HORSE PARADE, 1908

The annual Horse Parade shown passing St. Catherine's Plain. The wall of the Notre Dame Convent is on the left, and St. John de Sepulchre's Church is in the background.

The reverse side of the postcard has a pre-printed order form for Wilkinson's coal merchants, 46–48 Heigham Road, Norwich, with their depot at Victoria Station.

NORWICH CITY POLICE (1), 1914

The first of three postcards showing scenes from the annual inspection of the Norwich City Police held in Chapelfield Gardens in 1914. Eight members of the cycle contingent ready for inspection with their immaculate heavy-duty purpose-made police-cycles. Fourth from right is P.C.55 Cubitt Elvin, whose daughter still lives in the city.
In the background is the beginning of Vauxhall Street, and on the right, the corner shop belongs to Frank W. Utting, printer and tobacconist, 19 Chapel Field Road.

NORWICH CITY POLICE (2), 1914
The chairman of the Watch Committee, accompanied by the Chief Constable, E. F. Winch, inspecting constables of the Norwich City Police. Each constable holding his truncheon, handcuffs, whistle and chain for inspection.

NORWICH CITY POLICE (3), 1914
The sixteen men of the Mounted Branch of the City Police on parade in Chapelfield Gardens.
Police-horses have always been effective in crowd patrol. They were also used to marshal large numbers of cattle and
horses attending Norwich market.

UPPER HELLESDON MILL FIRE (1), 1913

Upper Hellesdon Mill stood in Press Lane, off Aylsham Road, and was owned by Mr. Ephtain Witard.
A series of ten postcards were published illustrating the events relating to the fire which destroyed the mill on 4th May, 1913. The first postcard in the series shows the City's first motorised fire-engine CL 67, purchased in 1911 for £948, about to depart for the fire. (These details were discovered by the author from a notebook belong to P.C. Cubitt Elvin, who also attended the fire in his capacity of part-time fireman; many policemen were members of the fire brigade at this time).

UPPER HELLESDON MILL FIRE (2), 1913

At the height of the fire, four firemen can be seen on an extended ladder, at the top of an adjoining building, directing
a jet of water through the upper windows.
The six other postcards not shown, illustrate various stages of the fire and the resultant damage to the mill.

UPPER HELLESDON MILL FIRE (3), 1913

Showing the aftermath of the fire: broken and smoke-blackened windows, the roof-less adjoining building, and the mill interior completely destroyed.
(See also Volume 1, page 104, which shows the mill before the fire).

UPPER HELLESDON MILL FIRE (4), 1913
One of the horse-drawn fire appliances returning from the mill fire, and shown passing Philadelphia School on Aylsham
Road.
Notice the ice-cream cart and pony by the tram standard in the centre of the picture; the pony appears to have been star-
tled by the speed of the passing horses!

A. J. CALEY & SON LTD., c. 1920

A. J. Caley & Son was founded by a local shopkeeper who produced mineral waters in his cellar. The business grew rapidly, but as the demand was seasonal, he also started to produce cocoa, which lead to chocolate. In order to find further employment for his female staff who made the boxes for his chocolate, he started manufacturing crackers. These three products became a major industry in Norwich. Between the two World Wars, A. J. Caley merged with John Mackintosh & Sons, which later merged with Rowntree's of York. Cracker making and mineral water production became separate industries. In 1988, after much local controversy, Rowntree's were bought by Nestlé's.

This is an unusual advertising postcard published by A. J. Caley & Son, Fleur-de-Lys Works, Chapelfield. Notice how the cows' tails spell MILK CHOCOLATE.

JACKSONS' FAMOUS HATS, p.u. 1907

A rare and very collectable advertising postcard by the famous cat artist, Louis Wain, produced for Jacksons of 20, London Street, who were still at this address in 1933.

An advertisement on the reverse of the postcard states:- "Our specialities: All one price — hats 3/9d; boots 10/6d; umbrellas 6/9d; raincoats 21/-. We beg to inform you that we have now received our Spring and Summer goods, and our stock comprises everything that is smartest and best in felt and silk hats, caps, umbrellas, raincoats and waterproofs, boots and shoes, etc. A visit would be esteemed".

The Lovers' Walk
Chapel Field Gardens

"THE LOVERS' WALK", c. 1912

A mass-produced comic postcard illustrated by 'Cynicus', pseudonym of Martin Anderson. Known as a stock card and overprinted to order for any location nationwide.
Courting in Chapelfield Gardens appears to have been rather crowded in those days!

In preparation: Norwich Volume 3;
A Third Portrait in Picture Postcards